Magdalyn's Heart

Written by
Amanda
Ball-Knight

WestBow Press books may be ordered through booksellers or by contacting:

WestBow Press
A Division of Thomas Nelson & Zondervan
1663 Liberty Drive
Bloomington, IN 47403
www.westbowpress.com
1 (866) 928-1240

ISBN: 978-1-9736-1794-5 (sc)
ISBN: 978-1-9736-1795-2 (e)

Library of Congress Control Number: 2018901255

Print information available on the last page.

WestBow Press rev. date: 7/3/2018

WESTBOW
PRESS®
A DIVISION OF THOMAS NELSON
& ZONDERVAN

Dedication

This book would have never come about without my Lord & Saviour Jesus Christ dealing with my heart and giving the inspiration to write it.

This book is also dedicated to my children, Maggye and Halbert.

1st Place for Kindness

4

"Rise and shine, Sleepyhead," Mom whispered softly as she pulled back the covers from Magdalyn's head. "It's time to get up and start your day!"

"UGH! Is it morning already? Just five more minutes!" Magdalyn grunted as she peered at her mom through squinted eyes.

"Yep! Such a beautiful day the Lord has made!" Mom said enthusiastically as she rustled Magdalyn out of bed.

It was like any normal day. Magdalyn got out of bed and changed out of her jammies. She brushed her hair.

Magdalyn ate her breakfast.

After breakfast,
Magdalyn brushed her teeth.

Then she headed
off to school.

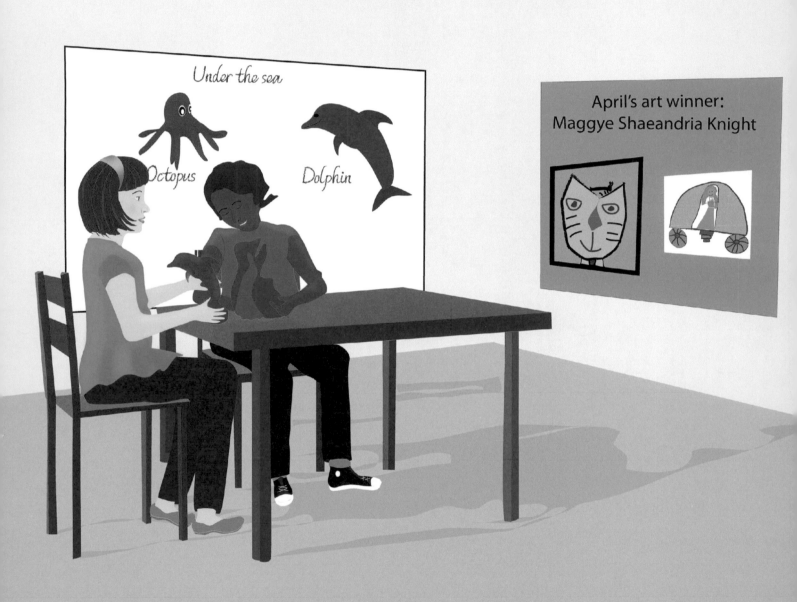

Magdalyn attended Eagle Elementary School. She loved school! Her favorite subject was art and her best friend was named Susie. The day was filled with reading island, spelling bees, and math assessments. There was also time for fun and games at recess.

All day Magdalyn was reminded of what her mom had said that morning, *"A beautiful day the Lord has made!"* Every time the thought crossed Magdalyn's mind her heart smiled! Although Magdalyn's heart would smile when she would remember this, she felt like there was an empty spot in her heart. She felt like someone was knocking on her heart.

14

The day was finally over and the bell rang. Magdalyn could hardly wait to get home. She wanted to talk to her mom about how her heart had been feeling all day at school.

As Magdalyn walked in the door she began talking with her mom. "Mom, my heart feels empty. I think Jesus is talking to me. I want Jesus to live in my heart." Magdalyn and her mom walked into the bedroom and sat down on the bed to talk.

"Do you remember the ABC's, we talked about in Sunday School?" Mom asked.

"Yes! Admit. Believe. Confess." Magdalyn explained.

"Let's talk about them." Mom pulled out her Bible and read a passage in Romans.

"That if thou shalt confess with thy mouth the Lord Jesus, and shalt believe in thine heart that God hath raised him from the dead, thou shalt be saved. For with the heart man believeth unto righteousness; and with the mouth confession is made unto salvation. For the scripture saith, Whosoever believeth on him shall not be ashamed. For there is no difference between the Jew and the Greek: for the same Lord over all is rich unto all that call upon him. For whosoever shall call upon the name of the Lord shall be saved." (Romans 10:9-13 KJV)

"We must admit we are sinners." Mom went on to ask, "Do you know what a sinner is sweetie?"

"Umm...yes, it's doing something that's not pleasing to God," Magdalyn answered.

"We also must believe! We have to believe that Jesus died for our sins," said Mom. "Do you remember the story of the Roman soldiers beating Jesus and then hanging Him on the cross?"

"Yes, it was so sad. Then the soldiers put Jesus in the tomb." After a pause Magdalyn continued, "But after three days Jesus was ALIVE!!"

"That's right! And do you believe with your whole heart that Jesus did that for you?" Mom asked.

"Sure do!" Magdalyn exclaimed.

Confess

"Once we have prayed the sinner's prayer and accepted Jesus as our personal Saviour we must confess it to the world. Do you know what the word confess means?" Mom asked.

"Uh...no. Not really!?!?!?" Magdalyn said, sounding confused.

"Confess just means to speak. So, in other words, we need to tell the world Jesus is our Saviour and not be ashamed of Him," Mom explained.

"Oh, I get it!" Magdalyn chimed in.

Mom grabbed Magdalyn's hands, gazed into her eyes, and asked her, "Do you feel Jesus speaking to your heart telling you it's time to be saved?"

With tears streaming down her cheeks Magdalyn replied, "Oh, yes Mommy!"

Magdalyn and her mom kneeled at the bedside. Mom prayed alongside Magdalyn as she asked Jesus to live in her heart.

Dear Lord,

I love you! Thank you for all you have done for me! Please forgive me and help me walk closely in your footsteps! Lord save me and live in my heart! In Jesus' name, Amen.

As the prayer ended, Magdalyn received everlasting salvation through Jesus Christ.

Special Acknowledgements

"Magdalyn's Heart" was illustrated by Nancy Salings. She enjoyed working alongside author Amanda Ball-Knight on this project. Nancy has won several awards for her art.

Special Acknowledgements

The book "Magdalyn's Heart" is based on the salvation story of Maggye Knight. Maggye is the daughter of author Amanda Ball-Knight and Joe Knight. Maggye spends her free time creating art. You can see two of her art pieces featured in this book on the classroom art winner bulletin board. These art pieces were featured in the Young Artist Art Showcase in the county where she resides. She was surprised and excited that artist, Nancy Salings, incorporated them into this book.

Printed in the United States
By Bookmasters